IMPROVING YOUR PERFORMANCE

Mark T. Barclay

All scripture references are quoted from the
King James Version of the Holy Bible
unless otherwise noted.

Second Edition
First Printing 1994

ISBN 0-944802-03-6

Write:
Mark Barclay Ministries
P.O. Box 588, Midland, MI 48640-0588

CONTENTS

Introduction

Conclusion

Prayer of Salvation

INTRODUCTION

I have titled each chapter of this book in order to establish a thought with you and cause you to investigate that subject. Then I have split the chapters into two sections. The first section is for pastors, and the second section is addressed to the flock. For example, chapter 5 of this book is titled "Authority." As you read that particular chapter, you will see that there is a small introduction followed by a section written to pastors and then a section to the flock.

In the introductory portion of each chapter, I will address the subject of the chapter as it relates to everyone. I will share scriptures here as well.

In the section for pastors, I will write the pastoral aspect of the subject and how pastors are to respond. I will be sharing from a pastor's heart, focusing on the other pastors.

In the section to the flock, I will be addressing and teaching the family of God in matters pertaining to their relationship with the pastor.

By using this method, each chapter should briefly do three things: It should basically cover the subject of the chapter along with scriptural support, it will address all pastors on the same subject, and it will show the family of God how to respond according to the Word.

As you read this book you will be able to see a little of both sides of the sheepfold. Prayerfully this will help you to work and flow together in the same mind and spirit.

Enjoy the book, and please allow the Holy Spirit to engrave His truths upon your heart.

CHAPTER 1
IDENTITY CRISIS OR CHARISMA?

"Paul, an apostle, (not of men, neither by man, but by Jesus Christ, and God the Father, who raised him from the dead;)"

Galatians 1:1

". . . I will come to visions and revelations of the Lord."

2 Corinthians 12:1

"Be ye followers of me, even as I also am of Christ.

Now I praise you, brethren, that ye remember me in all things, and keep the ordinances, as I delivered them to you."

1 Corinthians 11:1-2

"And my speech and my preaching was not with enticing words of man's wisdom, but in demonstration of the Spirit and of power . . ."

1 Corinthians 2:4

It is easy to see that Paul of Tarsus was not ashamed to speak boldly about who he was and what he was doing. The fact is, he spoke some very bold things such as, "Be ye followers of me" and "Keep the ordinances, as I delivered them to you."

These statements were almost blasphemous in the ears of religious people of his day. Even today people might call you proud if you were to go around speaking like this.

Humanity today seems to float from one fad to the next. People are patterning themselves after rock music groups, singing stars, and movie stars. They are into designer clothing, embossed and pictorial shirts displaying their favorite television show, and bumper stickers revealing their favorite sport or hobby.

It seems as though the whole world wants to be identified with something. People join clubs, societies, lodges, and foundations. They are comparing horoscopes, family roots, and ethnic beliefs. Many people drink a certain beer or wine because of its name. There are some who smoke a certain brand of cigars or cigarettes simply because of what the name of that brand implies.

People who are for strict economies and who pinch pennies will drive a small, compact car because they feel it represents the group they want to be identified with. Others want to drive a large, plush luxury car because it identifies them with yet a different group of people. Some dress in a cowboy style, some in a preppy style, some in loud checks and stripes, while others dress moderately.

Do you realize that humanity is in such an identity crisis that even things like hosiery, undergarments, jewelry, and wallets all have to be just the right style, color, and manufacturer in order to be accepted?

Has this hunger for recognition and identity entered into the body of Christ?

PASTORS

Unfortunately, the answer to that last question is a definite *yes*. I believe that it is one of the reasons why we have so many denominations today.

When pastors come together to fellowship, you are more apt to hear comparisons of ministerial style and performance rather than actual testimonies of the Lord's moving.

Pastors want to really advertise their church name, ministry name, and style in order to promote their product. Please don't misunderstand me. I think you ought to advertise your church to the public so that the believers will know you exist, and those in need will know where to get help. Unfortunately, many pastors are motivated differently.

Your identity should be associated with charisma rather than crisis. You leaders should be very comfortable in knowing who you are and what you've been commissioned to do.

What do I mean by charisma? I simply mean that you should always be identifying yourself with the Holy Spirit, the Bible, and the Head of the Church—Jesus. You should do your best to cause the people of God to relate to the entire body of Christ and world vision rather than just your local church and its particular vision.

People want to relate and belong to a church of good quality. People are normally excited and enthused rather easily. This is why many of the cults of our day grow so quickly and fool so many people. It is your place as local shepherds to orient the flock of God to the entire Church body. You must use the Scriptures as well as the gifts of the Spirit to display what you represent.

Okay, pastors, find your place and settle into it. Seek the Lord and determine, while in His presence, who you are, what you are, and exactly how He wants to use you in His Kingdom. Once this is done, absolutely nothing will sway you—not persecutions, rate of growth, financial conditions, or even part of your flock visiting neighboring churches.

Identify yourself, and stand up for what God has made you. Don't turn to gimmicks or worldly ways to promote yourself. Be honest, sincere, humble, and most of all—anointed. Look out! Whatever you identify with, so will your followers.

THE FLOCK

Come on, folks, don't be ignorant of the wiles of the evil one. Time is short. You need to establish your hearts and do something of quality with the remaining days of your life.

Don't be fooled by great advertising campaigns. Don't take any one man's word and govern your family by it. Search the Scriptures daily so you can be convinced of the true way.

Search and find a quality church that has a true man of God to pastor it. So what, if you have to drive an hour each way. So what, if they worship a little differently than what you are accustomed to. Big deal, if they receive several offerings in one meeting! It is all worth it.

You are going to identify with something. It's the

human way. Please don't let it be the flashy promises of a cult. Please don't let it be those fleshly hooks of social groups. Please don't let it be the stigma of carnality found in the great *religions* of today. Choose Christianity and the Spirit-filled Church. Choose to identify with those who are allowing the Bible to govern their vision and their church.

My number one suggestion to you as a member of the body of Christ is to find for yourself and your family a pastor who is void of gimmicks and who is led by the Spirit and the Word of God. Once you find such a man of God, support him with prayer, finances, attendance, and a heart of submission.

Please don't let your hunger for identification drive you into a worldly, lustful crisis. Don't live a life of pretense and facades. Turn that *identity drive* toward a life of charisma—being led by the Spirit of God, the Word of God, and a man of God.

CHAPTER 2
LEADERSHIP/LORDSHIP

"And I will give you pastors according to mine heart, which shall feed you with knowledge and understanding."

Jeremiah 3:15

"And he gave some, apostles; and some, prophets; and some, evangelists; and some, pastors and teachers;

For the perfecting of the saints, for the work of the ministry, for the edifying of the body of Christ . . ."

Ephesians 4:11-12

"Feed the flock of God which is among you, taking the oversight thereof, not by constraint, but willingly; not for filthy lucre, but of a ready mind;

Neither as being lords over God's heritage, but being ensamples to the flock."

1 Peter 5:2-3

What a matter of confusion this has been. For years people have had trouble defining the difference between leadership and lordship. There is a real misunderstanding in the body of Christ today over the words *shepherding* and *discipleship*. Especially in the charismatic realm, people tend to fear when a man speaks up and declares himself the leader. Why? Perhaps there is error in much of the teaching on the subject. Perhaps it is because of the great amount of carnality found in the leaders of these fellowships. Perhaps it is because of the "flighty," unsettled, insecure motivations of many Spirit-filled people.

There is a great misunderstanding in the body about the strong leadership—churches, and those who go by the "however we feel lead" program. To correct this error, many local pastors are standing up and declaring that they are to govern the church as the Lord Jesus directs them. This declaration seems so strong that many of the flock feel as though they are being lorded over rather than pastored.

PASTORS

Pastoring is taking on a new connotation today. They are beginning to submit to the heart of the Chief Shepherd. They are beginning to declare with their mouths that Jesus really has set them in a supernatural office in His Church. They no longer have to do things out of their own abilities or education. Best of all, they no longer have to do them all themselves. I stir you, pastors, to learn to lead that flock supernaturally. As you do, they will respond supernaturally.

In the Gospel of John, chapter 10, Jesus revealed to us two different styles of shepherding. He called one a true shepherd and the other a hireling. He explained that the true shepherd is like this: The good shepherd will not hesitate to give his life for the sheep. He knows his sheep, and they know him. He has the heart of God to pastor (a pastor's heart). Therefore, he has partial ownership of the flock. If anything happens to the flock, he loses part of his ownership, and a portion of his commission to shepherd becomes injured.

The hireling is totally different. He refuses to lay down his life for the sheep. When trouble comes, he will flee and abandon the flock. The sheep do not belong to him; rather, someone has simply hired him to feed or watch them.

Is the hireling less a man of God than a true shepherd? I guess that depends on how you look at it. Basically, they could both be very good Christian men. They could both love the Lord equally. What is the difference then? The difference lies with the appointment they receive.

A true shepherd has been appointed to the office by the Owner of the sheep. He is to shepherd the flock because he has been given partnership with the sense of partial ownership as an undershepherd. He is appointed to do this regardless of pay, conditions, or opposition.

On the other hand, the hireling is just the opposite. He has been *hired* by someone other than the Owner of the flock. Perhaps a board of deacons voted him in and struck a bargain with him to pastor the local church for so much money and benefits per month. When he was hired, he was given a certain prescribed amount of authority and duties. He will probably do his best to perform these duties but not much more. When trouble or hard times come, he will probably feel called to go elsewhere.

Please know that there are true men of God who were raised in or stuck in a hireling system. Many of them would function at peak performance if they could get free from the "deacon possessed" system that is robbing their ministry.

THE FLOCK

*"The prophets prophesy falsely, and the priests bear
rule by their means; and my people love to have it
so . . ."*

Jeremiah 5:31

*"And I will gather the remnant of my flock out of all
countries whither I have driven them, and will bring
them again to their folds; and they shall be fruitful
and increase.*

*And I will set up shepherds over them which shall
feed them: and they shall fear no more, nor be dis-
mayed, neither shall they be lacking, saith the LORD."*

Jeremiah 23:3-4

Listen to me, people of the Lord! It is God's plan that
you should have a pastor watching over you. You are
to worship the Lord, but you are to be submitted to your
pastor.

Jeremiah, chapter 5, verse 31 (which we quoted
earlier), tells the whole story. For the most part, the priests
(or pastors today) have ruled the Church through their own
means, and the people have loved it. This is evident.

When a pastor begins to rule by the Word of God and
the voice of the Holy Spirit, the people's first instinct is to
rebel. They always want to say things like, "Who does this
guy think he is, the Lord or something?" or "I have never
seen this kind of stuff done in any other church I've
belonged to," and on and on and on.

Most people were more comfortable sitting under a
pastor who ruled carnally. They don't like to be challenged
face-to-face. People don't like to be corrected or rebuked.

The majority of people who make up the average church expect the pastor to do the work. "After all, that's what we pay him a salary for!" These people really have a fit when a pastor comes to them and tells them what to do.

Take a good look at the following scripture, and I will show you what kind of things to expect from your pastor:

"And thou shalt teach them ordinances and laws, and shalt shew them the way wherein they must walk, and the work that they must do."

Exodus 18:20

Number one, your pastor should be teaching you the ordinances and the laws of the Lord—not just the *church* laws and ordinances. Number two, he should be showing you the way in which to walk. This is done by example and by training you. This is called making disciples. The third thing your pastor should be doing is supervising you in the work you must do. If you want more scriptural support of this, look to Ephesians, chapter 4, verses 11-14.

If God has ordained leaders over you and equipped them to lead, then He must be equipping you to follow.

Both you and I know that no man has the right to lord over your personal life and affairs. Jesus is Lord, and this is true for pastors and the flock. So if you've got a pastor who is taking the place of Jesus in your life and wanting you to worship or bow down to him, be careful. However, don't mistake supernatural leadership with unlawful lordship.

Simply said, Jesus has given the pastor authority to be a leader, and He has given you authority to be a follower. Let your pastor lead, and you submit. If only the body of Christ were as interested in themselves being submissive as they were in their pastors being a pastor, things would be much different.

A word to the wise—keep your nose in your own business. You work hard at being good little sheep, and the pastor will work hard at being a good little shepherd. Believe me, both will need a tremendous amount of help from the Lord.

Remember, God is the only One who sets supernatural pastors over you.

CHAPTER 3
A SUPERNATURAL LOOK

"But ye are a chosen generation, a royal priesthood, an holy nation, a peculiar people; that ye should shew forth the praises of him who hath called you out of darkness into his marvellous light . . ."
1 Peter 2:9

"Ye also, as lively stones, are built up a spiritual house, an holy priesthood, to offer up spiritual sacrifices, acceptable to God by Jesus Christ."
1 Peter 2:5

"For as the body is one, and hath many members, and all the members of that one body, being many, are one body: so also is Christ.

For by one Spirit are we all baptized into one body, whether we be Jews or Gentiles, whether we be bond or free; and have been all made to drink into one Spirit."
1 Corinthians 12:12-13

Today the Spirit of the living God is speaking very clearly to the Church to come away from religious ways and doctrines of men.

In the hearts of both pastors and flocks, a great message is being stirred by the Holy Spirit. What is that message? *Be supernatural in all you do.* To the pastors, God is teaching supernatural ways to shepherd the local flock. To the local flock, God is teaching supernatural ways to properly relate to the pastors and other sheep in the fold.

Finally, both pastors and their congregation are hearing from God and working together to fulfill the vision of the Lord and reap the great harvest of souls.

Here is the kind of church that Jesus had to deal with:

". . . The scribes and the Pharisees sit in Moses' seat:

All therefore whatsoever they bid you observe, that observe and do; but do not ye after their works: for they say, and do not.

For they bind heavy burdens and grievous to be borne, and lay them on men's shoulders; but they themselves will not move them with one of their fingers.

But all their works they do for to be seen of men: they make broad their phylacteries, and enlarge the borders of their garments,

And love the uppermost rooms at feasts, and the chief seats in the synagogues,

And greetings in the markets, and to be called of men, Rabbi, Rabbi."

Matthew 23:2-7

This pretty well defines what the Church once was and even what many tend to be today. Thank God that His Holy Spirit is challenging us to come away from this religiosity and be spiritual people.

14

PASTORS

One of the major satanic snares of pastors and leaders is pride or arrogancy.

This is exactly what the devil wants you to be—full of pride, a know-it-all, seeking the chief seats at the feasts, exalting yourself above the people. The enemy loves it when God's leaders get a little "puffy." All he has to do is squeeze them a little, and they spew out their many accomplishments and their list of personal achievements.

This is exactly what Jesus was telling the multitude and His disciples. He warned them to be careful of leaders who were not supernatural. He warned them to be on the alert for those leaders who press down hard on the Church and keep people servants of guilt and condemnation.

Jesus said these kinds of leaders always "say, and do not." Be careful, pastors, that you do not turn into a carnal dictator. Beware of discontentment and laziness on your part. Jesus also said that they do all of their works to be seen of men. Come on, leaders, who really cares what men think or say? If you will really examine yourselves, you will see that your inner man wants to be pleasing to God.

Don't get caught up in all the gimmicks, prestige, and superficial areas of the ministry. Stay humble, work hard, be a good example, and follow the Holy Spirit. You'll see that it is easy to be a supernatural leader.

THE FLOCK

Many people today are being saved and filled with the Holy Spirit right in the presence of denominational barriers and religious structure. The enemy has lied to many of these dear sheep and convinced them that they are to stay in their religious rut in hopes of converting the whole group. DON'T BE FOOLED, MY FRIEND!

One day a lady who was ill came to me and asked if our elders would anoint her with oil and pray the prayer of faith over her. I didn't recognize this person, so I asked her if she belonged to our fellowship. Her answer was very clearly, No. I wanted to know why she requested prayer from our elders if she was attending another local church, so I asked her. This was her response: "Oh, Brother Barclay, we have a lovely pastor and real faithful elders at our church, but they are not spiritual, and I don't have any confidence in their prayers."

How sad! She went on to tell me where she went to church and why she stayed there. Not one reason she gave me was at all scriptural. She so much wanted a supernatural pastor, but she was afraid to walk in that direction.

Another time a man came to me after a service in our church. He introduced himself and began to tell me how much he appreciated the church family here and all the great things he received during our services.

I had seen this man several times in our services, but he was not really steady in attendance. I began to inquire about his family, background, and church affiliation. This is what he told me: "I am born again and Spirit filled, but my pastor isn't. I don't get fed at all in the church I belong to, so I come here as often as I can to get spiritual food and encouragement. The reason I stay in my church is because I've been there for years and years. My pastor depends on me, and I don't want to let him down. Besides, I know that the Lord is going to use me to cause a revival in that place."

Here's what I told him: "You have been deceived!" When I asked him how many he had led to the Lord in the past year, he said, "None." That in itself was proof enough to me. I appreciate this man's loyalty, but I think it was charged with stupidity! How can a man admit that he has such a pastor (who is not born again or Spirit filled), and that he is not getting fed the Word but still take his wife and family to submit to that carnal, religious leadership. Sad to say, he will certainly reap what is being sown.

Listen to me, people of the Lord! Be led of God's Spirit. Hook up to a supernatural pastor and congregation, and do something with the rest of your life. Don't settle any longer for excuses and deceptions. Be brave!

FIND YOURSELF A SUPERNATURAL PASTOR, HOOK UP WITH HIM, AND DON'T LET GO FOR ANYTHING.

CHAPTER 4
CONSISTENCY

"And let us not be weary in well doing: for in due season we shall reap, if we faint not."

Galatians 6:9

One of the weaknesses of the Church today is a lack of consistency. It can exist in both the pastorate as well as in the local flock.

We seem to be living in a "do what you feel like doing when you feel like it" era. There is a great lack of spirit and fight in Christians today. Of course, this isn't true of everyone, but it certainly seems like the majority.

Please read the following passage of scripture taken from the Book of Joshua. It clearly shows us how we should perform as the army of God.

"And the armed men went before the priests that blew with the trumpets, and the rereward came after the ark, the priests going on, and blowing with the trumpets.

And Joshua had commanded the people, saying, Ye shall not shout, nor make any noise with your voice, neither shall any word proceed out of your mouth, until the day I bid you shout; then shall ye shout.

So the ark of the LORD compassed the city, going about it once: and they came into the camp, and lodged in the camp.

And Joshua rose early in the morning, and the priests took up the ark of the LORD.

And seven priests bearing seven trumpets of rams' horns before the ark of the LORD went on continually, and blew with the trumpets: and the armed men went before them; but the rereward came after the ark of the LORD, the priests going on, and blowing with the trumpets.

And the second day they compassed the city once, and returned into the camp: so they did six days.

And it came to pass on the seventh day, that they rose early about the dawning of the day, and compassed the city after the same manner seven times: only on that day they compassed the city seven times.

And it came to pass at the seventh time, when the priests blew with the trumpets, Joshua said unto the people, Shout; for the LORD hath given you the city."

Joshua 6:9-16

PASTORS

How would you like to be in Joshua's shoes? He told the people literally to "shut up and march." I can just imagine what would happen today if we had to keep all the sheep quiet!

Joshua told the people of the Lord not to shout, not to make any noise with their voices, and not to let any word proceed out of their mouths. This was a pretty strong decree coming from this leader.

I wonder how many of us pastors today would be strong enough to carry out such orders. Many leaders are afraid of the people. They see their congregations as a majority. You know, the tithers, deacons, elders, and their wives shouldn't be challenged, and especially don't tell the head deacon's wife to zip her lip—that is, if you cherish your position and don't want to be voted out of your office. Thank God that Jesus, the Head of the Church, placed me in this office of pastor and that He is the only one who can remove me.

Joshua not only told them to hush, but he even had the boldness to describe a marching order. He told them all where and how to march, even to the minute detail of who would stand where. Oh, how I pray for pastors to be consistent leaders. He listened to what God said, and nothing swayed him from accomplishing just that.

Regardless of the attendance each day, he marched the army of God around Jericho. I am sure people began to murmur and complain and lament about the leadership of this man of God. Can't you just see the people's reaction? Each day they all lined up and marched silently around the city God had given them. So they did for seven days.

Sure it looked silly. Sure the people questioned his leadership ability. Sure the enemy laughed at them as they marched by each day. But it was the consistency of this great man of God that kept the people marching decently and in order.

You and I know, pastor, that he must have had his hands full! We also know the great reward of being a consistent leader. Joshua's rewards were so tremendous, they are still spoken of today.

How about it, pastors? Are you men of God or men of men?

Tell your congregation that you are here to stay. Let them know that you have no plans to desert the flock. Show them by example that you mean business and that you are consistent.

THE FLOCK

You and I both know that no one likes to be told what to do. After all, this is a free country, and we have certain rights. How dare anyone try to tell us great Americans any differently. Besides, where the Spirit of the Lord is, there is liberty (liberty—yes, sloppy rebellion—no!).

You should keep in mind that you are more than an American. Thank God we had the privilege to be born and to live in such a supreme country. No one is more American than this author, but to a greater degree, I am a citizen of Heaven. I am not of this world, I only live in it.

Drawing your attention to the quoted scripture about Joshua, imagine what the people must have thought. Sure the leader had a tough job but so did all the others. It must have felt pretty silly to just keep marching around that city day after day, not saying anything.

Some people say, "I'd love to go to your church, Brother Barclay, but the reputation you have would label me in the community. You are pretty extreme about the Word, worship, giving, and all that. I need something more mild so people won't judge me so harshly." Okay, Mr. Compromise, God bless your business and your life . . . if He can.

I wasn't with Joshua and God's people the week they marched at Jericho, and neither were you. It's really hard to tell all that took place there. Even so, if the same order were given today, I know exactly what would happen. Most of the congregation would leave and join a new flock with a less radical leader. Upon the first command of the pastor to hush, they would pull out.

Those who remained would have a hard time listening and being obedient to the pastor's decree on where they were to fit in. Everyone would want to vote on the marching order.

I can see people marching the first day or two without too many problems. On the third, fourth, or fifth day, however, today's average Christian would now be murmuring, complaining, and judging the pastor's decrees.

On the sixth day, after all the heathen friends and the enemy had mocked them and teased them, most of the marching ranks would be thinned out. "After all, God doesn't expect us to go through this kind of stuff. Our pastor is just making a fool of himself and us. I don't want to drive my friends and family away." Where are you going to drive them to? Is there a hell number 2 or hell number 3? Of course not. Come on, believers. Rise up with consistency, and stop being ashamed of the gospel.

On the seventh day the marching ranks would be even thinner—especially after the fourth or fifth time around the city. "After all, if the pastor really heard from God, something should have happened by now."

You just grit your teeth, use your backbone, and follow that consistent, supernatural pastor around and around, and you'll be on the scene when God demonstrates His reward for faithfulness.

I can see it! The great day of victory comes after the seventh trip around the city on the seventh day. The walls come down, and all the people who were hooked up and stuck it out are rejoicing. It was worth it all.

Do you want to know what stinks to God, the pastor, and the victors? On the day of victory all the dropouts and quitters show up to take part in the celebration. They say things like: Didn't we do a good job of building this church? I just know the Lord is so proud of us. After all, God doesn't expect us to take on any more than we can personally handle.

Listen to me, people of the Lord. No one likes to be laughed at or persecuted. No one likes to keep plugging along when the opposition is rough. But for those who can be consistent enough, there is a supreme reward awaiting them!

What do you think? I'm for grabbing ahold of the vision of the Lord and marching very consistently until the old religious walls come down. The laugh is on the enemy. He's the one who looks shabby when the battle is won.

BE CONSISTENT!

CHAPTER 5
AUTHORITY

Authority is needed desperately in the Church today. A lack of it has hurt the body of Christ and caused many to be sick, poor, restless, lazy, and rebellious. All of us need to be governed properly, or we will lose the proper timing and momentum of the Lord.

Pastors need to be governed by the Head of the Church (Jesus) in order to function in His perfect plan. The congregation needs to be properly governed by their pastor (shepherd) in order to stay in one accord and be in God's perfect plan.

The devil likes to interrupt and pervert this flow of authority. He tempts leaders and followers to misuse authority, causing us to be independent and refusing to submit. God has put things decently in order. He has a chain of command for His purposes, and He simply expects you and me to fit into that line of authority.

PASTORS

It is very clear throughout the Bible that you have been delegated authority to be leaders over God's people. You are going to be held accountable for the flock that He has entrusted to your care. You are responsible for the well-being and safety of the sheep.

If you have been given the responsibility to guard, feed, and oversee His flock, then you are going to give an account of how well you do. If you are going to be held accountable for this responsibility, then Jesus is going to give you all the authority you need to fulfill your pastorate. It is not your authority but His. He has simply delegated it to you. You use it strictly by direction of His Spirit, His wisdom, and His Word.

Jesus was known for authority: "And it came to pass, when Jesus had ended these sayings, the people were astonished at his doctrine: For he taught them as one having authority, and not as the scribes" (Matt. 7:28-29).

When you begin to recognize this godly authority within you, it will show in the pulpit, your counseling, prayers, office management, public relations, etc. Believe me, pastor, the people will immediately notice it because you'll be so much different than the religious rulers.

Be sure to maintain the knowledge that this is Christ's authority, not yours. If you start decreeing things in the flesh, people will recognize the flesh and turn from you. Exercise that authority, according to the Word, and you'll see it become a powerful force in the ministry.

THE FLOCK

Please don't be afraid of authority. I am aware of as many men who have failed and led people astray as you are. Yes, I know about cults and crises where leaders have misused authority and many were hurt. These were not men of God. Please don't be afraid to submit to a man of God and allow him the opportunity of ruling over you in the church.

Remember—Jesus is a Shepherd, not a dictator. Therefore, He will rule you to the degree of your submission rather than by His force. The same is true with a supernatural pastor.

Is rulership really of God? Yes!

"And when Jesus was entered into Capernaum, there came unto him a centurion, beseeching him,

And saying, Lord, my servant lieth at home sick of the palsy, grievously tormented.

And Jesus saith unto him, I will come and heal him.

The centurion answered and said, Lord, I am not worthy that thou shouldest come under my roof: but speak the word only, and my servant shall be healed.

For I am a man under authority, having soldiers under me: and I say to this man, Go, and he goeth; and to another, Come, and he cometh; and to my servant, Do this, and he doeth it.

When Jesus heard it, he marvelled, and said to them that followed, Verily I say unto you, I have not found so great faith, no, not in Israel."

Matthew 8:5-10

This portion of scripture tells us that Jesus was impressed with the understanding that this man had of authority. The Bible says that Jesus marveled. It also shows us that Jesus had trouble finding this kind of faith in Israel. This revelation of authority moved Jesus, and He sent His Word and healed the centurion's servant.

"Let every soul be subject unto the higher powers. For there is no power but of God: the powers that be are ordained of God.

Whosoever therefore resisteth the power, resisteth the ordinance of God: and they that resist shall receive to themselves damnation.

For rulers are not a terror to good works, but to the evil. Wilt thou then not be afraid of the power? do that which is good, and thou shalt have praise of the same:

For he is the minister of God to thee for good. But if thou do that which is evil, be afraid; for he beareth not the sword in vain: for he is the minister of God, a revenger to execute wrath upon him that doeth evil."

Romans 13:1-4

"Render therefore to all their dues: tribute to whom tribute is due; custom to whom custom; fear to whom fear; honour to whom honour."

Romans 13:7

My friend, if you are doing good works and are pleasing in the sight of God, you have no fear. Relax and submit to the man of God. Submission is simply protection to the believer. God has set protective leaders over you. All you have to do is allow them to function in a godly manner.

You will see that by you and your pastor being scriptural, the authority of Christ will present itself in a marvelous manner in your presence. You just might be submissive enough to impress Jesus to tell your pastor to delegate some authority to you, thus making you a leader in the house of the Lord.

Remember that you will reap what you sow. As a new

leader, you will want to do everything right and be productive. But . . . if you were not submissive to your leaders, don't expect to reap anything different from your helpers.

The absence of Christ's authority is a personal invitation to the devil.

CHAPTER 6
HONESTY, HUMILITY, AND LOVE

What has the Church become without these three particular elements? For years we have seen ministers and others perform dishonestly, pridefully, and with partiality. The pastors have figured out the people, and the people have figured out the pastors. The result has been a basic distrust between leadership and flock, thus quenching and grieving the Holy Spirit.

HONESTY—Tell It Like It Is.

Why should any of us believe one thing and voice something different? What is gained by a smiling face and a bitter heart? Speak the truth with boldness.

HUMILITY—See It Like It Is.

We might just as well realize who and what we are. Everybody else does! Don't pretend to be someone else. Admit your faults, and strive to see yourself as God sees you. Don't cover up your mistakes or make excuses for your inabilities.

LOVE—Share It Like It Is.

True love includes friendship, edification, discipline,

and protection. Don't mistake this with the world's way of loving. A father truly loves his son as much when he is spanking him or rebuking him as when he is doing fun things with him.

> *"He hath shewed thee, O man, what is good; and what doth the LORD require of thee, but to do justly, and to love mercy, and to walk humbly with thy God?"*
>
> Micah 6:8

PASTORS

Volumes could be written on these subjects. There seems to be such a severe lack of these qualities in pastors today. You should pray that God continually reminds you to be supernatural leaders, keeping you out of the flesh.

HONESTY

Believe me, pastors, people want to hear it the way it is. Put your britches on, and go to the pulpit with boldness. You don't have to be afraid of the people. They love the Lord, and they love you. Your church will get nothing of quality done until you learn to be sweet, blunt, and very bold. You are their leader, so lead them!

If you have heard from God on a matter, then you should have all the confidence you need to speak up. Your old natural mind wants to convince you that you might offend the people or drive them away. This is a lie. The reason they are with you, most likely, is because they are hungry for the truth. Jesus had no problem displaying the truth. You are His representative.

HUMILITY

Don't cover up your mistakes, sins, or shortcomings.

You live in the same world the flock does. Relax! When you take a wrong turn or make a mistake, tell the people. You are their example. If you know how to confess and repent, it will help them. No, they will not lose respect for you. They probably saw you make the mistake anyway. I don't know about you, but I would rather follow a leader who knows how to correct himself and get back on course than one who is so proud that he never even sees his mistakes.

LOVE

Be like Jesus. Lead without partiality. This will be hard with close friends and especially family members in your fellowship. You don't owe any man anything but to love him. Let your love be without partiality. Be kind, polite, forgiving, longsuffering, and stable with all people. Your flock needs a pastor who will be like this even more than they need a teaching pastor. Of course, the supreme is to give them both. You can do it!

THE FLOCK

HONESTY

You aren't fooling anyone at all. You might just as well tell it like it is. Be specific and really clear where you stand. Please don't be found in a place similar to Ananias and Sapphira. When you are confronted by your church leaders, be quick to own up to the charge if you've faulted. Be without exaggeration if you are making accusations. Speak the truth with clarity to all of the church family, and you will be accepted. It will be the real you they are accepting.

HUMILITY

No . . . you are not God's chosen special agent to

humble the leadership of your church. No . . . you are not the great selected person of charisma whom God has set in the church with a special call to discern when the pastor is teaching truth and when he is in error. No . . . you are not the most mature, gifted, and spiritual person of the whole flock, so stop flaunting yourself, trying to impress everyone.

RELAX! Be yourself at home, in the church, and on the job. You are beautiful, and people want to get to know YOU! If they wanted to know that person you are pretending to be, they would just look back to what they were before they humbled themselves under Christ.

Don't pretend! Be you—the born-again, Spirit-filled, set-free you. We love you, and you are accepted. Don't build a relationship with us on the pretense of being someone or something you aren't. We'll soon see that it really isn't you, and we'll have to start all over.

LOVE

If you love Jesus as much as you say you do, then you will show it by taking care of the ministry *gift* He has given you. Love always gives. God so loved, He gave.

Believe me, flock of God, your pastor wants your approval, attention, and support as much as you want his. It means so much to him when you give properly, show up for church, and treat him scripturally. He is giving his life for you. What are you doing for him?

A WORD OF CONCLUSION

In order to walk in unity and be productive as the army of God, the body of Christ must have good leadership as well as good fellowship.

In order to be motivated and mobilized properly, there must be leaders who are capable of organizing the believers and keeping them in proper ranks. It is time for the body of Christ to be mobilized and go about doing what God has called them to do.

In this book, *Improving Your Performance*, I have shared those things that have helped me become a successful pastor as well as a mature man of God. You have seen that every chapter revealed basic scriptural truths on the characteristics of a supernatural pastor. Knowing that these qualities are in your heart is not enough. You must be able to live by them and develop them in other people.

Whether you are the pastor or not, you are responsible to God to do what He wants you to do and be what He wants you to be.

My prayer for you is that you retain the portions of this book that pricked your heart and that with all godliness you work together as a team.

Blessings upon you as your relationship between pastor and flock becomes one of unity and divine love.

Jesus will be pleased, and He will be in the midst of you.

PRAYER OF SALVATION

YOU CAN BE SAVED FROM ETERNAL DAMNA-TION and get God's help now in this life. All you have to do is humble your heart, believe in Christ's work at Calvary for you, and pray the prayer below.

"Dear Heavenly Father:

I know that I have sinned and fallen short of Your expectations of me. I have come to realize that I cannot run my own life. I do not want to continue the way I've been living, neither do I want to face an eternity of torment and damnation.

I know that the wages of sin is death, but I can be spared from this through the gift of the Lord Jesus Christ. I believe that He died for me, and I receive His provision now. I will not be ashamed of Him, and I will tell all my friends and family members that I have made this wonderful decision.

Dear Lord Jesus:

Come into my heart now and live in me and be my Savior, Master, and Lord. I will do my very best to chase after You and to learn Your ways by submitting to a pastor, reading my Bible, going to a church that preaches about **You**, and keeping sin out of my life.

I also ask You to give me the power to be healed from any sickness and disease and to deliver me from those things that have me bound.

I love You and thank You for having me, and I am eagerly looking forward to a long, beautiful relationship with You."

Books by Mark T. Barclay

Beware of Seducing Spirits

This is not a book on demonology. It is a book about the misbehavior of men and women and the seducing/deceiving spirits that influence them to do what they do. Brother Barclay exposes the most prominent seducing spirits of the last days.

Building a Supernatural Church

A guide to pioneering, organizing, and establishing a new local church. This is a fast-reading, simple, instructional guide to leaders and helps people who are working together to build the Church.

Charging the Year 2000

This book will remind you of the last-days' promises of God as well as alert you to the many snares and falsehoods with which Satan will try to deceive and seduce last-days' believers. "A handbook for living in the '90s."

Enduring Hardness

God has called His Church an army and the believers, soldiers. It is mandatory that all Christians endure hardness as good soldiers of Jesus Christ. This book will help build more backbone in you.

How to Avoid Shipwreck

A book of preventive medicine, helping people stay strong and full of faith. You will be strengthened by this book as you learn how to anchor your soul.

How to Relate to Your Pastor

It is very important in these last days that God's people understand the office of pastor. As we put into practice these principles, the Church will grow in numbers and also increase its vision for the world.

How to Always Reap a Harvest

In this book Brother Barclay explains the principles that make men successful and fruitful. It shows you how to live a better life and become far more productive and enjoy a full harvest.

Improving Your Performance

Every Christian everywhere needs to read this book. Even leaders will be challenged by this writing. It will help tremendously in the organization and unity of your ministry and working force.

Preachers of Righteousness

This is not a book for pulpiteers or reverends only but for all of us. It reveals the real ministry style of Jesus Christ and the sold-out commitment of His followers—the most powerful, awesome force on the face of the earth.

The Real Truth About Tithing
With the extremely fast lifestyles of these last days, it leaves little time to thoroughly study God's Word. When you finish this book, you will be fully equipped and informed to tithe properly and accurately. All of your tithing questions should be answered. Your life will never be the same.

Sheep, Goats, Wolves
A scriptural yet practical explanation of human behavior in our local churches and how church leaders and members can deal with each other. You will especially enjoy the tests that are in the back of this book.

The Sin of Familiarity
This book is a scriptural study on the most devastating sin in the body of Christ today. The truths in this book will make you aware of this excess familiarity and reveal to you some counterattacks.

The Sin of Lawlessness
Lawlessness always challenges authority and ultimately is designed to hurt people. This book will convict those who are in lawlessness and warn those who could be future victims. It will help your life and straighten your walk with Him.

The Making of a Man of God
In this book you'll find some of the greatest, yet simplest, insights to becoming a man or woman of God and to launching your ministry with accuracy and credibility. The longevity of your ministry will be enhanced by the truths herein. You will learn the difference between being a convert, an epistle, a disciple, and a minister.

The Remnant
God has always had a people and will always have a people. Brother Barclay speaks of the upcoming revival and how we can be those who are alive and remain when our Master returns.

The Captain's Mantle (minibook)
Something happened in the cave Adullum. Find out how 400 distressed, indebted, and discontented men came out of that cave as one of the most awesome armies in history.

Basic Christian Handbook (minibook)
This book contains basic doctrines that are simple yet necessary to every Christian's walk with God. It will be a vital help to new converts in the Kingdom. This also makes a great tract or altar counselor's tool.